On the
Teaching of
Creative Writing

WALLACE STEGNER

On the Teaching of Creative Writing

Responses to a series of questions

Edited by
Edward Connery Lathem

Montgomery Endowment
Dartmouth College

DISTRIBUTION BY THE
University Press
of New England

Kenneth and Harle Montgomery Endowment
Dartmouth College, Hanover, New Hampshire

The informal commentary by Wallace Stegner
published within this volume is based upon and
extends from tape-recorded discussions engaged
in by him before Dartmouth audiences, with
Professors Jay L. Parini and A. B. Paulson and
with Visiting Author Ishmael Reed, during Mr.
Stegner's period in residence at the College as a
Montgomery Fellow in June and July of 1980.

Composition and printing by
The Stinehour Press

Design by the Editor

Frontispiece: Dartmouth College photograph of
Wallace Stegner in 1980, by Nancy Wasserman

Distribution: University Press of New England
23 South Main Street, Hanover, New Hampshire

On the
Teaching of
Creative Writing

creative… Specifically of
literature and art, thus also of
a writer or artist: inventive. . . ,
imaginative; exhibiting imagination
as well as intellect, and thus
differentiated from the merely
critical, 'academic', journalistic,
professional, mechanical, etc.,
in literary or artistic production.
So *creative writing*, such writing;
also frequently in the United States
as a course of study.

—*A Supplement to the
Oxford English Dictionary,*
Volume I (1972), page 673.

What, Mr. Stegner, is your reply to the question of whether creative writing can, in point of fact, be "taught"? —

⚜ W. S. ⚜ That question has been coming at me, as you can imagine, for a long time, because I taught writing for something like forty-four years, before retiring.

I remember a time, years ago, when I dined with the dons at Magdalen College, Oxford. They stood me up and filled me as full of arrows as St. Sebastian. I presume they all believed that writing must be learned—that it is a gift that needs developing and disciplining—but none of them believed that it is a legitimate subject for a university course.

All I could say in answer was that they lived under privileged conditions. In England, a small country the size of some American states, a young writer can go to London, frequent the right Hampstead pub, meet literary people, begin to do a few of the chores of literary journalism—a book review here, a little article there, a poem, a critical essay—and in that way begin a literary apprenticeship.

The United States is too big a country for that. New York, in spite of the fact that it is the publishing capital, is not a literary capital, in the sense that London or Tokyo or Vienna is. Some young writers—Tom Wolfe, for an example—do throw themselves into that surf and try to swim. Others do not; many cannot.

So, for many Americans who grow up

in the provinces, as I did, there is no convenient and inevitable place to go to make contact with other writers and with the writing establishment, the general technology of writing. Most regional capitals, at least until recently, have been culturally impoverished or undeveloped. The best alternative has been those minor centers that exist in colleges and universities. In the circumstances, their development has been inevitable.

Within the academy, of course, there are limited things that a teacher can do, apart from encouraging the environment of interest and criticism within which writing can take place. How can anyone "teach" writing, when he himself, as a writer, is never sure what he is doing?

Every book that anyone sets out on is a voyage of discovery that may discover nothing. Any voyager may be lost at sea, like

John Cabot. Nobody can teach the geography of the undiscovered. All he can do is encourage the will to explore, plus impress upon the inexperienced a few of the dos and don'ts of voyaging.

A teacher who has been on those seas can teach certain things—equivalents of the use of compass and sextant: the language and its uses, and certain tested literary tools and techniques and strategies and stances and ways of getting at the narrative essence of a story or novel or the dramatic force of a play or the memorableness of a poetically honed thought.

Any teacher can discourage bad (meaning, unproductive or ineffective) habits and encourage those that work. He can lead a young talent to do what it is most capable of doing, and save it from some frustrating misdirections. He can communicate the necessary truth that good writing is an end in itself, that an honest writer is a member of a worthy guild. That may be the most important function of the teacher of writing.

Within the academy, which is itself a sort of monastic sanctuary in the cultural darkness, he can encourage—and perhaps create a substitute for the places that more developed societies have created: the Mermaid Taverns and Hampstead pubs. In a university, people of similar interests and comparable talents can get together and knock sparks off each other.

In my experience, the best teaching that goes on in a college writing class is done by members of the class, upon one another. But it is not automatic, and the teacher is not unimportant. His job is to manage the environment, which may be as hard a job as for God to manage the climate.

Is it the case that everybody can be taught to be a creative writer? And should everyone be? —

⟨ W.S. ⟩ No, on both counts. I have always tried to keep in mind Ring Lardner's remark that you can't make a writer out of a born druggist. You can't make a sprinter out of a 250-pound hammer-thrower or a musician out of someone who is tone deaf. You begin with a gift, big or little, and you try to help it become whatever its potential permits.

It is a fact that many people don't know their own potential, and without help will never have a glimmer of what it might be. It is a sadder fact that some misread their potential and aspire to be something which their gifts simply don't allow them to become.

Nevertheless, I believe that talent is more common than we think, that it is all over the place, and that almost everyone has some degree of it—something worth developing. That does not mean that you can count on producing writers, the way an engineering school can count on producing engineers.

Writing is not a function of intelligence or application. It is a function of gift—that which is given and not acquired. All any teacher can do is work with what is given.

But I do believe that everyone born should have a chance to become the best he is capable of and that many have undeveloped or obscured gifts that, like spores, will grow if they are given water.

What does one look for in trying to determine whether an individual has any real potentiality as a creative writer?—

❦ W. S. ❧ One looks for signs of gift: obviously perceptiveness, alertness to the observed world, a feel for language. It is not easy, and different kinds of writers display very different stigmata of gift.

If you looked only at the feel for language, you would never predict that Theodore Dreiser, say, would become an important writer. The fact is, Dreiser had everything a novelist needs *except* the feel for language. He became an important novelist without having the ability to write an English sentence. So, prediction is a very dicey matter.

At Stanford we dealt with hundreds of applicants for fellowships. Candidates wrote a letter saying what they hoped to do, and sent along a sample of what they had done. I remember one year when I picked up two application letters together.

One was full of pretension, metaphysical conceits, strained metaphors, flowers of rhetoric. It was Faulkner crossed with Tristan Tzara or Monty Python—so turgid that one strained for its meaning—and it was four pages long.

The other one was four lines long. It said only that what spoke to this candidate, in our program, was its willingness to give every talent a chance to be itself; she hoped to write stories and hoped to write them well.

The second candidate's name was Tillie Olsen, and she did write stories, and write them well. We gave her a fellowship, and did not give one to the other applicant, because what spoke to us from her letter was directness and honesty, and what spoke to us from his was pretension and self-consciousness. He wanted, terribly, to be "literary." She wanted to write stories.

Not all prediction is as easy as that, and all such decisions are harrowing to make, because they mean so much, so personally, to the people you make them about.

Ultimately, what one looks for is sensibility—which need not be as effete as it sounds—and sensibility is essentially *senses*. One looks for evidence that eyes and ears are acute and active, and that there is some capacity to find words for conveying what the senses perceive and what sense perceptions do to the mind that perceives them.

What one looks for in language is not mechanical perfection of syntax. What one looks for is accuracy, rightness, vividness. And beyond that, of course, some notion, however rudimentary, of the seriousness of good writing, some sense that literature should enhance life.

Can individuals be given tutelage in creative writing at too early an age?—

❦ W. S. ❧ There is, surely, no age too early for the development of sensibility, and enough poets have lisped in numbers, to make me believe that there is no age too young for writing.

The apprenticeship for poets is likely to be shorter than for fiction writers, because (at least in our time) poetry is essentially lyrical, which means personal, and the person is aware of himself well before he is fully aware of his entanglement in a society and a culture—the sort of entanglement out of which fiction most often arises.

So, there is no "legal age" for indulging the itch to write, but there may be a certain minimum age when one may expect the results to be memorable. Poetry matures younger than prose; individuals and sensibilities are very different.

But there may well be such a thing as

teaching writing too early. Teaching implies a personality, in the student, that is at least half-formed. It also involves—I wish it didn't, but it does—a certain validation of the student's ego. Young writers test themselves against the opinions of others, and especially against publication. Putting something in print is an enormous maximation of the literary ego.

I have known teachers who made junior-high and high-school students offensively literary, by persuading them that what they wrote was better, more mature, more worthy than it was. They have helped encumber children of fifteen with vast expectations, sure to be disappointed or long postponed, and that seems to me an ill-service. Students that young should be encouraged and challenged; they should not be inflated with false hopes.

The literary apprenticeship, despite the

contrary evidence of certain precocious individuals, is normally long. Most fiction writers are not really writers until their late twenties or even later. And the maturing process cannot be taught, it has to happen.

You can write your head off when you are in college or for a few years afterward, and people may praise what you do, but nobody is likely to want to publish it. Then, suddenly, someone does want to publish something. You can't see any difference between it and the things you were doing two or three years ago, but some editor can. You send him the earlier things, hopefully, and he sends them back. But he wants the new one, and perhaps other new ones after it. Something unpredictable has happened in your head or on your typewriter, and no teacher did it—though a teacher may have helped it along.

A long answer to a short question. A

shorter answer would be: Young writers should be encouraged to write, and discouraged from thinking they are writers. If they arrive at college with literary ambitions, they should be told that everything they have done since their first childhood poems, printed in the school paper, has been preparation for entering a long, long apprenticeship.

At least in the beginning, that apprenticeship does not have to be served in a classroom. Letters can be part of it, journals, anything that will force the expression of experience in words.

Does that suggest, then, the appropriateness of urging students to gain experience with life, before they seriously attempt any pursuit of writing?—

Ⓦ W.S. ☾ If you have to urge a writing

student to "gain experience with life," he is probably never going to be a writer. Henry James has some useful advice in this regard. He urges young writers to be people "upon whom nothing is lost." But in another essay, one on Maupassant, he is dubious about Flaubert's celebrated instruction to observe the cart horse until you can render him distinct from every other cart horse on earth.

Note-taking, James suggests (and he was himself a great note-taker, so that his advice may be ambiguous), is hardly the best way. You don't go out and "commit experience" for the sake of writing about it later; and if you have to make notes on how a thing has struck you, it probably hasn't struck you.

The people who are really going to be writers don't need urging to pay attention to their lives and experience. Experience strikes them. Even James, whom one critic describes as having proceeded through his life from inexperience to inexperience, was never in any doubt when one of his inexperiences was memorable. He was one of those upon whom nothing, even an inexperience, was lost.

Any life will provide the material for writing, if it is attended to. Willa Cather said that a novel is what happens in this room, today. I think it is. No urging is necessary. The ones who are going to do something will know what struck them.

But you yourself once declared, "Any work of art is the product of a total human being." And you have also emphasized that success in literature is not simply "a matter of mere verbal facility." Do those observations not suggest that a creative writer must possess, as background

for exposition and expression, a relative matur-
ity of experience? —

🙶 W.S. 🙷 Oh, sure. Of course. I didn't
mean to imply that James's inexperience
was *really* inexperience or that any writer,
especially a writer of fiction, can write out
of his head, out of pure abstract invention.
He can't *invent* without experience.

What I meant was that experience
sought for the sake of writing about it may
produce reporting, or travel books, but it
is not likely to produce literature. And experience is of many kinds, some of them
so subtle and quiet it takes a good Geiger
counter to detect them.

The way to gain experience is to live,
but that does not mean one must go slumming for the exotic or outrageous or ad-
venturous or sordid or, even, unusual.
Any experience, looked at steadily, is likely

to be strange enough for fiction or poetry.

By the same token, the individual who has lived deeply and widely—and I mean lived, not gone slumming or adventuring for literary purposes—has more to write about, and perhaps a better base for mature wisdom, than someone less privileged.

And yet, I don't know. What did Thoreau know? He lived deeply in Walden, deeply in books, deeply in his mind. By occupation he was nothing spectacular, part-time surveyor and handyman.

The subject of fiction is not just what one did yesterday. It may borrow from the experience of others than the author.

Robert Frost used to say that a fiction writer should be able to tell what happened to himself as if it has happened to someone else, and what happened to someone else as if it had happened to himself. That puts the emphasis where it belongs: on the technique of communication, the persuasiveness of the fiction.

In your judgment, what is it that most needs to be done for students? —

⟨ W.S. ⟩ They need to be taken seriously. They need to be assured that their urge to write is legitimate. And, even when they must be discouraged from wasting their lives in a hopeless effort, they must not be dismissed flippantly—these are hearts you are treading on.

Every student has a right to be listened to and be told honestly whether what he has written strikes no sparks or few or many. Before a teacher tells anyone he is good, and has that magical promise, he had better make sure of what he is saying; before he discourages anyone, he had better remember how intimate a thing writ-

ing is and how raw the nerves that sur-
round it.

There are no special techniques for any
of this. This is part of the Socratic burden
of teaching writing. It is more an attitude
than a technique.

*Do you consider reading to be an important part
of the preparation for writing?* —

⟨ W. S. ⟩ Oh, definitely. Absolutely. We
learn any art not from nature, but from
the tradition, from those who have prac-
tised it before. Hemingway said you can
steal from anybody you're better than. But
you can steal—in the sense of being influenced by and, even, improving upon—
those who are better than you, too. People
do it all the time.

You can hear Joyce in Dos Passos'
U.S.A., and Dos Passos' *U.S.A.* in

Mailer's *The Naked and the Dead*. Writers teach other writers how to see and hear.

The possibility that illumination will come to your mind straight from personal experience is about as likely as that a boy will show slick basketball moves without having watched or played with older boys in some playground.

Furthermore, what influences you will change with time. You begin, after all, with what your taste and intelligence and experience will permit you to begin with.

I have heard T. S. Eliot say that the way to inculcate a love for poetry is to let young people begin with what moves them, the *Lays of Ancient Rome* or some such narrative, swift, easily comprehended, and easily remembered poetry. If a youngster has let "Horatius at the Bridge" or "The Battle of the Lake Regillus" work on him, he is pretty sure to go on to something harder and more rewarding—Eliot himself, perhaps, or Wallace Stevens or Rilke or whoever.

It goes without saying, too, that those who *hear* a lot of poetry in their youth are likelier to become poets than those who do not.

Though it is always helpful to the young to be steered and guided toward what may catch their interest, I would be inclined, also, to throw open the library and let them find many things for themselves. The delight of discovery is a major pleasure of reading; and discovery is one of the best ways to light a fire in a creative mind.

Imitation, of course, is a potential danger. There is commonly a stage in any writer's life when the influence of some admired writer shows. But imitation wears out fast. No talent that amounts to anything is likely to be encumbered with it long. And the talent that doesn't amount to anything can only be helped along for a certain distance, anyway.

Actually, it is remarkable how wide and varied is the reading of most of the writers I know. They read for curiosity, for the purpose of keeping an eye on the competition, for the pleasure of discovery in their own field. But they also read archaeology, biography, history, physics, geography, the revelations out of biochemistry labs. Anything that is intelligible to an intelligent layman is a way to the understanding of the world they live in and write about.

Some of that is the activity of active and curious minds, for the sake of the activity. Part has a practical usefulness.

A fiction writer, in particular, has to be a jack of all knowledges. If his fiction involves an Episcopal wedding, he has to know or find out the Episcopal marriage service, not to mention the Episcopal state of mind. The most casual acts of his characters may touch areas outside his own immediate experience, and states of mind other than his own. So, he reads, not committing reading for the sake of the information, but picking up all sorts of information in the course of reading that is done with only curiosity and interest for its motivation.

Then, should instruction in creative writing be concerned, at least in some part, with the handling of factual matter, of information? —

⊲ W. S. ⊳ Yes. There is no substitute for really knowing what you are talking about. The books with staying power are the ones that speak from large knowledge and add something to a reader's comprehension. But it is sometimes possible, and perhaps even legitimate, to fake, too.

You remember the Indian who was chasing the rabbit? He chased the rabbit because he hadn't eaten for three days. And he was very persistent; he chased the rabbit up and down and across, until he finally cornered him. Then, as he was fitting an arrow and drawing back his bow, the rabbit sat up and said, "Arf arf!" The Indian was astonished, and eased up on the bow and said: "What kind of rabbit are you? Are you really a rabbit, and are you *barking* at me?" "Oh, I'm a rabbit, all right," the rabbit said, "but in a tight place it's well to be bilingual."

In a tight place in a novel it is well to be bilingual, too. It is necessary to be able to fake. We all do it—vamp in a bass and cover up our deficiencies, with an air of confidence.

Nevertheless, there is generally no substitute for knowing what you are talking about. Many fictions, whether they involve history or some aspect of contemporary life not in the common experience, or science or small-town politics or the techniques of fighting forest fires, represent more knowledge, both from experience and from research, than shows on the surface.

This, too, is something that should be taught to a class, if only to dissipate the vulgar error that writing is easy, because it only involves "making words." Words must be *about* something, and making them isn't easy, by a long shot. It is not a frivolous pursuit. It should be taken as seriously as the search for the replicating machinery in the DNA of the *E. Coli* virus X170.

Rigor is what we are talking about, a responsibility to a certain kind of truth and to observed reality. The worst writing classes with which I have had any experience have been the soft ones—the mutual-admiration societies in which whatever is said, if it is said well, is right. A teacher who permits that sort of atmosphere to develop gives his students a profoundly wrong impression of the profession and of the professional's obligations.

Once or twice I have taken over a class after it had been handled for a term by a soft and indulgent teacher who gave everybody A, exacted no penalties for late work or no work, and uncritically accepted the "truth" of what was written by his students. Those teachers were good people and good writers, but they were not good teachers of writing, because they demanded too little. After one term under their direction, the class was spoiled; winter term and spring term were wasted time. Students get no benefit from that kind of indulgent teaching. Their only hope is to recover from it.

Would you speak next about the teaching of the "craft" aspects of writing, such as literary devices or techniques? —

⊚ W.S. ⊚ The question of how much "craft" one should and can teach is always open, as is the question of how directly and systematically one should teach it.

It is fatal (though by no means unheard of) for a teacher to impress his own craft, as well as his own conceptions, upon his students. It is, however, common practice to send a student out to learn a particular technique by studying a particular writer who was good at it: Joyce, say, for stream of consciousness or Conrad for the tricks of multiple narrators.

But I have never found it very useful to do this in a vacuum, just as a general exercise. If a student is struggling with a story involving narrators within narrators, he obviously should know *Lord Jim*. If he wants to report experience in the undifferentiated, unaccented flow of a consciousness, he must know Joyce, Dorothy Richardson, Virginia Woolf, and some other people. Maybe they will only teach him how not to proceed, but that is something.

I believe the need should give rise to the assignment—that, actually, the merest hint, in the discussion of a manuscript, is enough to send the young writer to the places that might be instructive. Abstract rules of technique are not useful unless someone has an occasion for their use, and finds himself deficient.

I have never believed in assigning an entire writing class a certain body of reading. That will do for literature classes, where the problem is different. But a writer is a whole individual, stealing from whoever can help him, and ranging all of life and literature for his clues. Assigning him set readings would be like sending a young Dalí or Braque or Monet to copy the "Mona Lisa" or "Blue Boy." It would be a way to make academic writers, not good ones.

Many of the best clues to craft come out of the class manuscripts under discussion. A telling phrase, an evocative paragraph, a swift clue to character, can be rolled on the tongue and rung on the table—and perhaps do more than Milton can.

Should the teacher, in the process of instruction, consciously try to shape a student's personality or to enlarge him or her as a human being? —

🎕 W. S. 🖜 Well, I have some fairly strong feelings about that. I do not believe I can teach anybody how to be a bigger or better or more humane person. But I do subscribe to the notion that in order to write a great poem one should be, in some sense or other, a great poet. That suggests that any writer had better be concerned with the development of his personality and his character.

I don't believe, with Oscar Wilde, that the fact that a man is a poisoner has nothing to do with his prose. It does have something to do with his prose. A poisoner will write a poisoner's prose, however beautiful. Even if it has nothing to do with private life, personal morality, or his general ethical character, being a poisoner suggests some flaw somewhere—in the sensibility or humanity or compassion or the largeness of mind—

that is going to reflect itself in the prose.

Most artists are flawed; but they probably ought to make the effort not to be. But how do you teach people to enlarge themselves in order to enlarge their writing? It is a little like asking them to "commit experience" for literary purposes.

Largeness is a lifelong matter—sometimes a conscious goal, sometimes not. You enlarge yourself because that is the kind of individual you are. You grow because you are not content *not* to. You are like a beaver that chews constantly because if it doesn't, its teeth grow long and lock. You grow because you are a grower; you're large because you can't stand to be small.

If you are a grower and a writer as well, your writing should get better and larger and wiser. But how you teach that, the Lord knows.

I guess you can suggest the *ideal* of it, the notion that it is a good thing to be large and magnanimous and wise, that it is a better aim in life than pleasure or money or fame. By comparison, it seems to me, pleasure and money, and probably fame as well, are contemptible goals.

I would go so far as to say that to a class. But not all of the class would believe me.

Have you any observations to make on adherence to a working regimen or routine, which is often cited as a discipline necessarily associated with being a writer? —

⟨ W. S. ⟩ Different kinds of writers devise different strategies. My own experience is primarily that of the novelist, and a novel is a long, long agony. When Bill Styron described it as like setting out to walk from Vladivostok to Spain on your knees, he was not just making a phrase.

You must submerge in a novel—or *I* must. It must be real to you as you work at it, and the only way I know to make it real is to dive into it at eight in the morning and not emerge until lunchtime. Then, for the space of each working day, it can be as real as the other life you live—the one from lunch to bedtime.

I know no way to become convinced, and stay convinced, of the reality and worthiness of a novel but to go out every morning to the place where writing is done, and put your seat on the seat of the chair, as Sinclair Lewis advised, and keep it there.

It is not an easy discipline for everyone. Young writers often rebel against it, because when they go off by themselves, day after day, they get restless.

It is the dullness of writing that they

must invoke; they must actively seek it; they must put themselves in a prison and stare across a typewriter at a wall for four or five hours a day, seven days a week. It had better be seven, too, not six, not five — certainly not two or three.

Nocturnals may find the quiet of past-midnight a better time than morning. Poets and playwrights and short-story writers, accustomed to bursts of intense work, will not need this long concentration. But everybody will benefit from a good, deep, well-worn, and familiar rut.

It is a good test of the depth of one's commitment, actually. Nobody can make you go there except yourself, and you will make yourself go there only because that is where you want to be, that is what you must be doing.

From the teacher's personal standpoint, are

there any special dangers against which he or she must be on guard? —

⊙ W. S. ⊙ There are several. One is that concern about students' work will crowd out application to your own. It is fairly easy for teachers of writing to become ex-writers.

Another is that the necessarily different preoccupations and approaches of successively newer generations of writers will lead the writing teacher into a cosmetic youthfulness—into imitation of his students—and lead him to forget what his own life has taught him. It is exhilarating, but often dangerous, to give up your own hard-won ground and try to gain stamping-space on someone else's.

Finally, there is the problem of extended foster-fatherhood. Young writers may come to depend on a teacher they respect;

and because they think of him as the one with experience, connections, and answers, they may continue to lean on him — perhaps for life.

Once committed to the parental role, a teacher can be swamped — in the pleasantest way possible — by old friendship and by the desire to help these young people whom he has known as beginners. Their collective need can swallow his whole life. It really can.

That is one reason I quit teaching. And even after quitting, I can't escape it. In more than forty years of teaching, I collected a lot of ex-students; and because I had the luck to be able to pick them for talent, an extraordinary number of them are publishing writers. I get to read a lot of galleys.

To what extent should the teacher try to become

internal to what students write, internal to their actual creative process of writing? —

☉ W. S. ☉ The internal part is the student's own business. Only he or she knows what is intended; only he or she can perform or realize it. A teacher should understand that intention, but not try to control it. He doesn't have to invent this young writer, he only has to help train him.

There are, of course, plenty of writing teachers who create cliques and coteries. I find them reprehensible—the wrong kind, bent on producing clones of themselves or their cult figures.

Negative capability, a phrase that Keats used, is what is needed here: sympathy, empathy, a capacity to enter into another mind without dominating it. Strong-minded teachers with narrow views of their function are more likely to give a student attitudes he must live down, than help in assuming his own full stature.

If our colleges and universities are today, as you have indicated, this country's principal centers for the teaching of creative writing, how has that circumstance come to be the case? —

❦ W. S. ❧ Writing instruction is something that did not exist in our colleges until the 20th Century. So far as I know, the other countries where it occurs have copied it from us. In some countries it still doesn't exist.

It began with Dean Le Baron Russell Briggs of Harvard, who early in the century began teaching a class that required a daily theme. (Those were the hard old days, before rigor was relaxed.) Many, many American writers came out of Dean

Briggs' class—and at least one of them, Robert Benchley, went on writing daily 800-word themes all his professional life.

Charles Townsend Copeland, also at Harvard, followed Dean Briggs' lead. Between the two, they must have trained half the American writers of their time.

Later, in the 1940s, when I was teaching at Harvard, Theodore Morrison created five positions in the writing section of the English department, called "Briggs-Copeland Faculty Instructors of English Composition," commemorating the role that Briggs and Copeland had played. By that time, of course, writing instruction had been carried to the farthest corners of the country. It was a staple, though minor, offering at the University of Utah when I was a student there in the 1920s.

The second step in a movement which has been progressive for a good many years was the founding of the Breadloaf Writers' Conference at Breadloaf, Vermont, one of the summer campuses of Middlebury College. That, the first of its kind so far as I know, stemmed pretty directly from Harvard—though Robert Frost and John Farrar of the publishing firm Farrar, Straus were principal founding fathers.

Farrar was the first director, but was soon succeeded by Morrison, who ran it for years, with a teaching staff drawn partly from Harvard and dominated, for those years, by Frost, Bernard DeVoto, and Louis Untermeyer. That staff gathered for two weeks at the end of every August to make academia and bohemia work in harness. They lectured, read manuscripts, conducted seminars and workshops, played a lot of tennis, drank too much.

If Breadloaf had lasted one day longer each year, the whole mountain would have blown up. But for fourteen days, the effects were often salutary. Young writers got all the stimulus they could stand; staff gave until they were drained.

Breadloaf became a model for many other conferences, many of them in regional centers—some in mountain resort areas, such as Aspen and Sun Valley and Squaw Valley.

A third development began in the fall of 1930 at the State University of Iowa in Iowa City, when Norman Foerster established something called the "School of Letters," including an early version of the writing program that has become the biggest and one of the best known in the country. Foerster made it possible for a graduate student in English to get an M.A. by submitting a creative thesis—stories or poems or a novel. (I was a graduate student at Iowa in that year, and I took that option. If I was not the first creative M.A. in the country, I was one of the first two or three.)

Foerster's program went so far as to offer the Ph.D. for a creative dissertation, too; but during the Depression that did not seem like a safe teaching credential, and some of us steered away from it, in favor of more orthodox degrees. Most writing programs these days offer the M.A.—or, more likely, the M.F.A.—but stop at that, believing the Ph.D. is properly a degree in literary history or literary criticism (preparation for teaching, not writing, but literature).

Nevertheless, beginning with Dean Briggs' daily-theme course and coming to a climax with the Iowa program and its imitators, writing had moved into the academy in a big way. As late as the end of the Twenties, the customary way for a writer to get his apprenticeship (both in experience and in actual writing) was to begin as a newspaperman. Many did it. Sinclair Lewis, Dreiser, Hemingway—and, before them, Howells and Mark Twain and Richard Harding Davis and Stephen Crane—all wrote their way off newspapers and into books.

It is very different now. Because in America it has never been easy for writers—and especially for serious writers—to make a living by their writing alone, many have had to seek backlog jobs. The revolution that put writing into the colleges created a lot of jobs, and they were particularly desirable because they could be for only a term or two—and in every case involved a three- or four-month break in the summer.

College programs also bred a new lecture and reading circuit. The result is that nearly every American writer you can name is associated either with some academy or with the academic lecture-platform circuit.

Writers used to be somewhat contemptuous of the colleges, and college English departments used to look with some suspicion on writers, as underbred wild men. Now the relationship is Cold War at worst; more often, a cold truce; and in some happy cases, a warm collaboration. Whatever the relationship, colleges are where most of our writers can be found.

Do you favor having, as is now typically the case, creative-writing instruction centered within English departments? —

ⓒ W.S. ⓢ As I have said, the relationship

isn't always smooth. English departments have, with some grumbling, made room for writers, feeling (sometimes with justification) that these people can sling words but are lacking in both learning and culture. The writers, on the other hand, often take the view that English teachers are disappointed writers, that they teach because they can't *do*, and that envy and jealousy are behind their resistance to the full academic acceptance of writers.

I think that, with time, those prejudices wear away. Poetry and fiction are normally accepted as publications that warrant the promotion of their authors, and there are some English departments whose principal claim to distinction is their writing section.

One thing should be said. No matter how warmly an English department welcomes a writing program, it should not have full control of it, especially of the selection of its writing teachers.

English departments are notorious breeding places for cliques and coteries. Their professors, if they are not mainly trained in the same graduate schools, are trained in the same system, and by scholars who are not infrequently systems-makers. Their training, moreover, is in reading, criticism, literary history — not in writing.

When they are allowed to pick writing teachers, they often pick what I feel are the wrong kind: esoterics, cult figures, bearers of some advanced or arcane True Faith.

I believe that the catholicity of a writing program, and the flexibility of its teaching, is better served by writers picked by their fellow writers.

Has our literature been influenced, in any particular manner or to any appreciable extent, by the fact that the teaching of creative writing has, here in America, been so preponderantly centered within colleges and universities? —

⊙ W.S. ⊙ That is hard to say. The writing that goes on in colleges and universities, both by students and by teachers, is likely to be as free from commercial pressures as writing anywhere. And that is both a safety and a danger, for whatever one may say about commercial pressures, they do squeeze out some of the lunatic fringe.

A coterie within an English department does just the opposite — encourages the experimental (and, sometimes, lunatic), with the assumption that it is "purer" than the writing that has publication as its goal. English departments' writing programs are not always hermetic, but there is that danger.

I doubt that the fads which sweep English departments—everything from the New Humanism to Reductionism—have much effect on the actual writing of the country, which is incorrigibly closer to life than the fads are.

But it is possible that a discerning critic might find in the literature of the last four or five decades—the period during which writing has established itself in our schools—a greater tendency to split hairs, a somewhat greater openness to the formation of "schools" (in the European sense), and a somewhat greater willingness to "experiment"—experiment being generally imitation of Joyce, who otherwise has not had an enormous influence on the art of fiction in America.

How, precisely, would one go about actually setting up a program in creative writing?—

⟨ W. S. ⟩ I had to grapple with that problem when I moved from Harvard to Stanford, at the end of World War II. Suddenly, I was surrounded by G.I. students just out of the armed services, much more mature than the ordinary college student, with many more things to write, and with a sense of urgency brought on by three or four years of lost time in the army or navy.

What could I do, in a provincial university, three thousand miles from New York and an hour from San Francisco, that would help and encourage these obviously gifted people? I had the experience of Harvard, Iowa, and the Breadloaf Writers' Conference, as well as the example of the Hopwood Awards at the University of Michigan, to guide me; and I borrowed from them all.

First of all, I wanted fellowship money, to buy some time for these writers. That has been the function of Guggenheim and other fellowship programs, and it needs no further justification.

Next, on the model of the Hopwood Awards, I thought we needed prizes; and we set them up. Later we abandoned them, because they bred a too-virulent spirit of competition, and because the problem of finding able and distinguished judges became too difficult.

Next, we needed money for some visitors, writers of distinction who could be brought to the campus for a day or a week or a term. Over the years we brought Robert Frost, Katherine Anne Porter, Elizabeth Bowen, Hortense Calisher, Walter Van Tilburg Clark, Frank O'Connor, Malcolm Cowley, and many more—some of them several times. They added immensely to the program. Like the fellowships, they turned out to be essential.

What else did we use our money for? Beyond fellowships, visitors, and the soon-abandoned prizes, nothing much — a little aid in publication, to put into book form the stories and poems produced by the annual crop of young writers.

The rest of the program was pretty standard English-department routines: a ladder of courses, from beginner to graduate, all taught by writers; and the privilege of submitting a group of stories or poems or a novel, as an M.A. thesis.

If you have gifted students — and we have never lacked them at Stanford — that is about all you need.

That leads to the consideration of what really does happen within the classroom of a creative-writing program? —

⟨ W.S. ⟩ Certainly one function of a

writing class is to lift students out of classroom amateurism and bring them into contact with professional aims and attitudes, either in the person of the teacher or of a visiting writer or of the members of the class themselves—or, sometimes, in books. The best possible justification for a writing class is that it should make students competent to deal with the word in all its manifestations.

As Robert Frost used to say, people have to know how far to trust a metaphor. Trust it too far, and it can break under you—and teach you the perils of analogy. That and many other things are best learned in the laboratory of pen, paper, and wastebasket; and in a writing class all the members are utilizing that lab simultaneously.

Another thing you may learn in a writing class is the ability to take and profit from criticism. How do you react when your cherished eloquence falls on deaf ears? At the very least, you should make a note that there are different kinds of ears and that what seems obvious or eloquent to you is dull or common to another sensibility.

I have had students who could neither give nor take criticism, without getting fiery red in the face and rough in the voice—so sensitive to personal slight that they could neither take it themselves nor dish it out, without a heavy component of hostility. Untreated, that disease can be fatal; even treated, it is uncomfortable.

If criticism affects you that way, you are very unlikely to "make it" as a writer, because there is no way to learn, except through criticism—your own or someone else's.

A writing seminar exerts criticism ad hoc upon a specific manuscript. A member of the class provides the subject matter, the class the discussion, the teacher no more than a mild Socratic guidance. Instead of a lecture, what goes on is a discussion which, with luck, may lead to some sort of illumination or consensus.

It is very difficult to do, actually. After two hours of apparently mild semi-participation, the teacher can come out feeling as if he had carried a piano up the stairs.

Sometimes, too—and this happens even to some of the most talented students—the class has a tendency to think of writing as spasmodic activity, and the class likewise. They are young people, full of hormones and themselves and other concerns, and they like a good time as well as the next person. Moreover, unless they are special students, taking only writing, they have plenty of other work to do.

It is, therefore, sometimes hard to keep

enough copy coming in to keep the class—especially if it is a small class—running. If there is no copy, we might just as well adjourn. That generally shames a class into getting busy, and helps develop the working habit that is probably the most important habit any writer needs to have. He has to learn it for himself, but a class that acts as a deadline—a hard deadline—can help him do it.

What else? A teacher can quietly squelch public confession (which is tempting to some writers) and public exhibitionism (which is just as tempting). The class itself is likely to do it for him. After all, if you "spill your guts" on the floor, you have to expect people to step on them—and that can be educational; it can teach you either not to spill your guts or to follow Frost's advice, and spill them as if they belonged to someone else.

By and large, a good writing class functions like a form of publication. Abruptly, this manuscript—this thing that was a scribbled page—is put into a posture of dignity, demanding attention. A tableful of people have listened to it; you yourself have listened to it, have heard yourself read it. It has been tested by both eye and ear, and is being tried now by this group whose opinions you may not always agree with, but have to attend to.

Merely having a story read aloud and discussed makes it, in its author's eyes, more serious and more worthy. And that group around the table may be the best audience, though not the biggest, that that writer will have in his life.

Publication itself, of course, carries the process much further. No piece of writing is fully real until it is published. Merely seeing it in a type face that is not a typewriter face will do it. *This* was actually set up by a printer and run through a press. Marvelous! And *I* did it. Suddenly, it is three times as important as when it was only a typescript.

Every writer who "makes it" at all has that experience. But it may be a long time coming. Publication through a reading in class is the next-best thing—and far more immediate. It will probably happen several times to each member of a class during the term, and it will ultimately separate the men from the boys.

The essentials are only two: taking a piece of writing seriously; and criticizing it with a view to helping it be what it wants to be. It cannot be done without some degree of abrasion. You don't sharpen a knife on a cake of soap.

You have said it is the teacher's task to "manage

the environment" of a writing class. Would you speak now about how that is achieved? —

⊙ W.S. ⊚ Managing the environment for a group of talented (and frequently headstrong) people is not easy. I have often thought of it as comparable to the way one trains a hot-blooded colt, whose whole impulse is to run. You put him in a corral and you let him run—in circles, with a rope on him. You don't yank his head off, and you don't let him run over you. You teach him to run under control. And much of his control is going to be learned from the other horses in the corral.

A writing class is inevitably competitive, do you see? Everyone's primary concern is his own success, and that success, when something as personal as literature is involved, is acutely personal. But if you encourage competition, or let it run rampant, any individual's success becomes everyone else's envy.

Ideally, if the class mix and the teacher's wisdom operate right, every individual's success becomes everyone else's stimulation. The people in such a class, if it is well selected, are roughly equal in talent and opportunity. If one puts a story in *The New Yorker* or gets an enthusiastic acceptance of his novel, other members of the class have a right to feel that the possibility is all the more available to them.

That successful one is no better than I am, they will think. The gift there is different from mine, but not superior. What happened to him is bound, sooner or later, if I work, to happen to me.

For some such reason, in seminars that jelled properly, I have seen people write better than they will ever write again — write better than they really know how to.

The trick is to keep the competitiveness friendly, to see to it that individual success stimulates other members of the group, instead of depressing and discouraging them.

What about the creative-writing teacher's concerns centering upon grammar and syntax and the like? —

☙ W. S. ❧ There are two kinds of teaching at issue here. One of them is the plain instruction—often the corrective instruction—in the communication of meaning through language. That goes on in "Freshman English" classes and in the kind of exposition courses often offered to engineers and other professional trainees.

It is absolutely essential—the white man's burden—and it is never done well enough. It has its basis in grammar and syntax, which are simply the logic of the language. (No two languages have quite the same logic, but each within itself is consistent.)

Inevitably, that kind of teaching has a certain place in a creative-writing course. I take it as a basic principle that anyone who aspires to use his native tongue professionally and publicly had better know it. I have spent a lot of time going over manuscripts with students, in the way an editor might go over them, to clean them up and make them presentable, and keep the author from appearing in public with his shirt tail out and egg on his tie.

That is not the truly important matter, but it is one of the things that can be taught, and it is not trivial—though young writers, full of fire and the will to unbridled originality, sometimes think it is.

Grammar and syntax are more important in fiction than in poetry, which can proceed by daring leaps. When a fiction writer dissolves grammar, syntax, and logic, he is in grave danger of dissolving everything he is trying to communicate. If he cannot be restrained or directed, he must be permitted to go his way, but he had better know what he is risking. If he tells me, "Don't try to figure it out, just groove on it," I am at least going to make it difficult for him to get away with it, without an argument.

So, whether dismembered syntax has sprung from ignorance or from the lust after originality, I believe it should be questioned. After all, all a reader knows is the marks on the printed page. Those marks have to contribute meaning—every meaning the story or poem is going to have.

We are dealing with a complicated symbolic system, and every element of that system, down to the conventional signs for pauses and nuances, has had a long testing. Its function is to help reproduce in cold print what was a human voice speaking for human ears. The system can be challenged—and, even, cracked—but it is challenged at the writer's peril, and he had better know it before he undertakes to change it. A good writing class can help him discover what works and what does not.

A final question, Mr. Stegner: Beyond developing a student's technical proficiencies and the influencing of his or her literary awareness, sensitivity, and understanding, can the teacher of creative writing actually induce or evoke talent —really cause talent to come into being?—

❦ W. S. ❧ A teacher probably can't, but a class sometimes can. No, let me qualify that. Talent can't be taught, but it can be awakened—by reading, by contact with other talents, by exposure to an environment where the expression of talent is valued and encouraged. And once it is awakened, it can be guided—unless it happens to be too headstrong, as it sometimes is. (If it is absolutely headstrong, it must be allowed to go its own hard way.)

I cannot say often enough that the teaching of writing is Socratic. The end is not the production of clones of any approved style or writer—and certainly not of the teacher! The end is the full development of what is unique in the young writer, without encouraging him in mere eccentricity.

Writing is a social act, an act of communication both intellectual and emotional. It is also, at its best, an act of affirmation—a way of joining the human race and a human culture. And that means a writer must have a clear conception not only of the self, but of the society.

After all, the language itself is an inheritance, a shared wealth. It may be played with, stretched, forced, bent; but I, as a writer or teacher, must never assume that it is mine. It is *ours*, the living core, as well as the instrument, of the culture I derive from, resist, challenge, and—ultimately— serve.

But, no, nobody can teach anyone else to have a talent. All a teacher can do is set high goals for students—or get them to set them for themselves—and, then, try to help them reach those goals.

A college class seems to me one of the best places for that sort of guidance.